Hacker's Guide To 35,000,000 Products

Alibaba.com: The Etsy, eBay and Amazon Treasure Chest

By Sam Sommer

Discover A Whole New World

Copyright, Legal Notice and Disclaimer

This publication is protected under the US Copyright Act of 1976 and all other applicable international, federal, state and local laws, and all rights are reserved, including resale rights: you are not allowed to give or sell this book and the materials contained in it, to anyone else.

Please note that much of this publication is based on personal experience and anecdotal evidence. Although the author and publisher have made every reasonable attempt to achieve complete accuracy of the content in this book, they assume no responsibility for errors or omissions. Also, you should use this information as you see fit, and at your own risk. Your particular situation may not be exactly suited to the examples illustrated here; in fact, it's likely that they won't be the same, and you should adjust your use of the information and recommendations accordingly.

Any trademarks, service marks, product names or named features are assumed to be the property of their respective owners, and are used only for reference. There is no implied endorsement if I use one of these terms. All images in this book are readily available in various places on the Internet and believed to be in public domain. Images used are believed to be used within the author's and publisher's rights according to the U.S. Copyright Fair Use Act (title 17, U.S. Code.)

Finally, use your head. Nothing in this book is intended to replace common sense, legal, or other professional advice, and is meant to inform and entertain the reader.

Copyright © 2017 Sam Sommer storm@ctaz.com All rights reserved worldwide.

Introduction

On Sept 18, 2014, in New York City, A Momentous Event Took Place

A company – The Alibaba Group, went public and raised almost one quarter of a trillion dollars in one day through a stock offer

It's founder, Jack Ma, instantly became one of the richest men in the world

When he was told, years ago, that he was not capable of managing a Kentucky Fried Chicken fast food restaurant, it did not faze him!

His companies will become the first to reach a trillion dollars in online sales

For years people put down one of his businesses – alibaba.com

YouTubers claimed the site could not be trusted, it was a rip off, products were cheap and unreliable, your money would get stolen – the list goes on

Some eBayers and Amazon sellers paid attention to this chatter, they never ventured forward. However, those that knew how to safely use the web site, made millions

Jack Ma at the Alibaba.com headquarters in China

35,000,000 Products To Choose From – Over 2,000,000 Suppliers

**Let me ask you two questions: Are You Sourcing From Alibaba.com?
If Not - Why Not?**

Did you know that a large number of top sellers on Amazon, eBay and Etsy, whose revenue exceeds $500,000 per year, source many, and sometimes all of their products, from Alibaba.com. Why this source? It's simple: they have branded themselves on eBay, Amazon and Etsy and import Chinese made products that are appealing, sell well and have great profit margins.

In This Book I Will Show You How To:

Safely source products from Alibaba.com and AliExpress.com (Alibaba's sister site)

What products to buy and what not to buy

How to identify trustworthy suppliers

How to brand yourself so you get higher search rankings

How to go inside eBay and Amazon to determine the most searched and best selling items

The only way to pay for product

How to determine if freight charges are fair – and much more!

Table of Contents

Alibaba – Meet The Giant

Let's Take A Look Inside Alibaba.com

The Alibaba.com Wholesale Site

Let's Look Inside AliExpress.com

Is It A Good Product?

Finding A Product To Sell

Buying A Product To Sell

Evaluating Products

Buying Samples

Paying For Your Products

Branding Increases Cash Flow

How eBay Sellers Make Millions Sourcing Alibaba Products

Conclusion

Alibaba - Meet The Giant

Now that the dust has settled from Alibaba's IPO (Initial Public Offering) we can clearly gaze upon one of the world's largest publicly traded companies. The IPO was a record for the U.S. Stock Market, the initial private offering raised $25 billion. On the first day of trading Jack Ma, Alibaba's founder, became one of the world's wealthiest individuals. Not bad for a former school teacher and someone who was told he was not qualified to manage a Kentucky Fried Chicken restaurant. By day's end, after the public stock was sold (Thursday Sept. 18, 2014), well over $200 billion came in.

To get a perspective on the size of this company and its future potential, here are some interesting facts to consider:

- **Alibaba has more employees than Facebook and Yahoo combined – over 20,000**
- **In 2013, it generated over $240 billion in sales from just two of it's web sites – more than twice the sales Amazon generates and three times eBay's**
- **It experienced three times the sales of our Black Friday, almost $6 billion, on the Chinese version of Black Friday**
- **It has almost 3 million suppliers and over 35 million products for sale**
- **There are over 230 million active buyers using Alibaba portals**
- **Just take, for example, their web site, Tmall: over 200 million people per month visit and use the site**
- **Now add to the equation the fact that half of China's population is not yet on line, and Alibaba will easily become the first ecommerce company to generate over $1 trillion in sales**

The companies that Alibaba own cover a wide range of financial interests. In this book we are only going to focus on Alibaba.com and AliExpress.com, as sourcing sites for product resale on eBay, Amazon and Etsy. The next image shows all of its holdings and what each is involved in. It is important to realize that Alibaba has a very strong foundation and a wide range of business assets:

There's an Alibaba for that

Alibaba Entity	Deals in	Is kind of like
Alipay	Online payments	PayPal
Aliyun	Cloud services	amazon web services
Aliyun App Store	Mobile apps	Google play
Aliyun OS	Mobile OS	android
AutoNavi	Maps and navigation	Google maps
InTime	Retail outlets	JCPenney
Juhuasuan	Group buying	GROUPON
Kanbox	Cloud storage	Dropbox
Laiwang	Mobile messaging	WhatsApp
Lyft, Kuaide	Car service, ride sharing	UBER
Taobao	C2C e-commerce	eBay
Taobao Travel	Online travel booking	ORBITZ
Tmall	B2C e-commerce	amazon.com
TutorGroup	E-learning	KAPLAN
Weibo	Microblogging	twitter
Xiami	Music streaming	Spotify
Youku Tudou	Streaming video	hulu

Quartz | Nikhil Sonnad — Data: Quartz analysis

As you can see from this list, Alibaba has tremendous diversity and balance. This list does not even include AliExpress.com and Alibaba.com. While most of these sites are unfamiliar to the Western World, many companies outside China are placing their products on Alibaba's platforms and taking advantage of their income potential. Our focus will be on Alibaba.com and AliExpress.com as product sourcing sites.

Alibaba.com is typically described as a business 2 business site, where you as a business owner buy product at wholesale prices for import and resell on sites like Amazon. AliExpress.com is a retail site, allowing anyone to buy product in single increments, unlike Alibaba.com, which focuses on larger purchases at much lower prices but does allow small purchases to help you get started. Individuals can purchase on either site and you do not need to verify yourself as a business entity in order to do so.

It is important to have faith in Alibaba as a company, because it has received bad press over the years. Sites like YouTube are not very complimentary. Typically people who have had bad experiences on Alibaba.com record their frustrations, often telling horror stories of how they got cheated and how products purchased were sub standard. These issues still occur today but they are becoming much less of a problem. Have no fear, you can buy quality product from reputable vendors on these sites. I have done it, and I will show you how.

Let's Take A Look Inside Alibaba.com

Alibaba.com has the look and feel of many commerce web sites that you have seen but some of its features stand out and are unique. Let's cover some basics. The next image shows part of the home page of Alibaba.com. I put a box around the sign in/join tab:

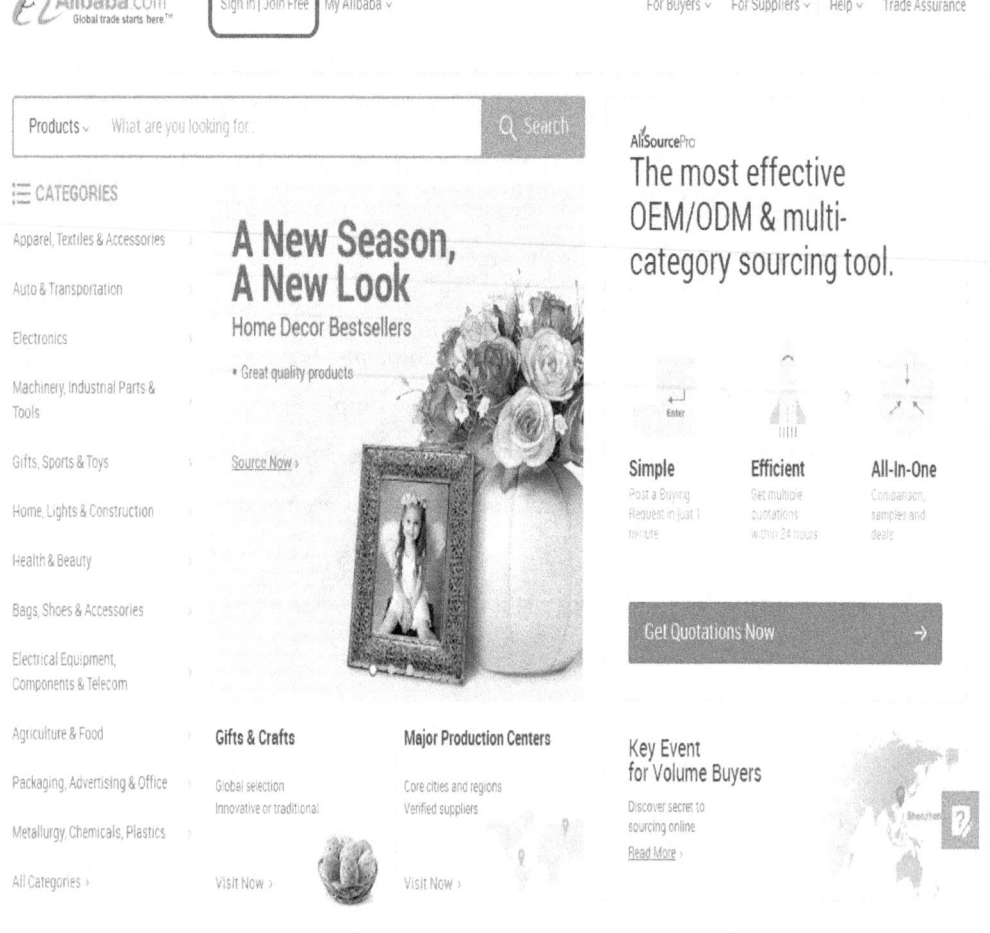

As you can see on the home page there is a search tab, a join free option, categories, and a category sourcing tool. The first thing you will want to do is join the web site, it is free and easy. If you click on the join free tab another screen pops up:

Alibaba.com
Global trade starts here.™ Account Registration

Create Your Account

*Email: [   ] This will be used to sign-in to Alibaba.com

*Create Password: [   ]

*Re-enter Password: [   ]

*Business Location: United States
--Province/State/County--

*I am a: ○ Supplier ○ Buyer ○ Both

Add your Contact Information

*Contact Name: [First Name] [Last Name]

*Company Name: [   ]

*Tel: [1] - [Area] - [Number]
e.g. 86 - 571 - 12345678

*Code shown: Ocu

Create My Account

Joining is simple and requires only your email address, password, country, state, buyer-supplier option, name, company name and phone. Don't worry, no one will call you. If you do not have a business name, make one up (take your last name and add & associates to it, for example: Jones & Associates). You do not have to enter any form of payment. Joining makes it possible for you to get product quotations.

When you click on the Category tab, up pops (next image), a list of available categories in alphabetic order and sub sets of each category. Look at Food & Beverage, the number next to it indicates that there are almost 2 million products in this sub category alone. One person cannot look at all the products on this web site in the span of a lifetime.

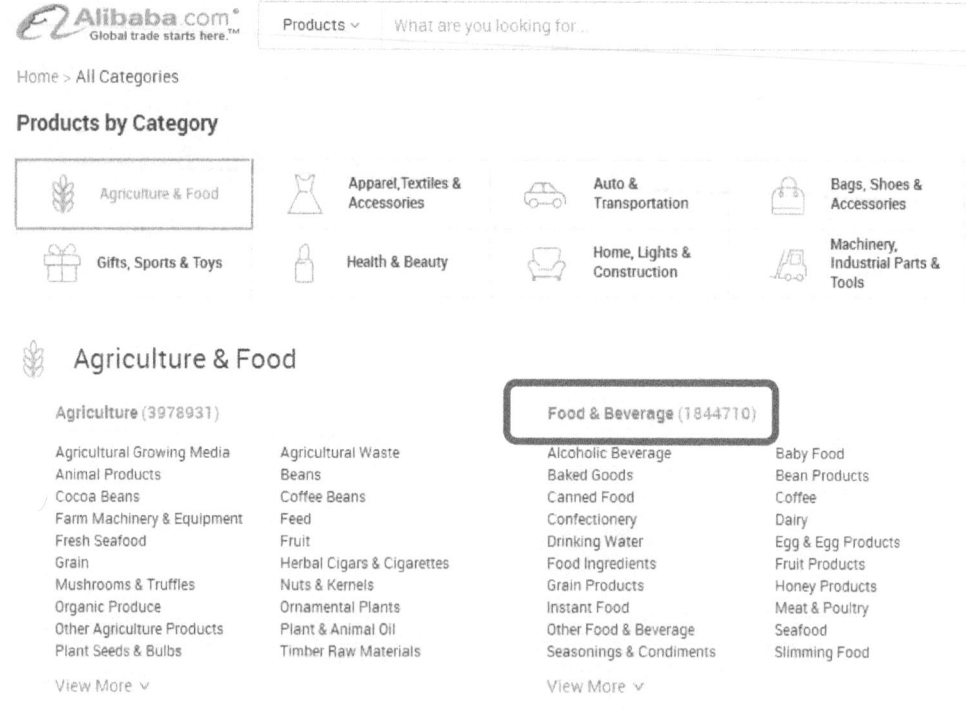

Fortunately for us Alibaba.com has created a tool that makes it easier to source products. A blue tab on the Home page: **"Get Quotation Now"**, brings up this screen: (I put the word "Projector" in the space)

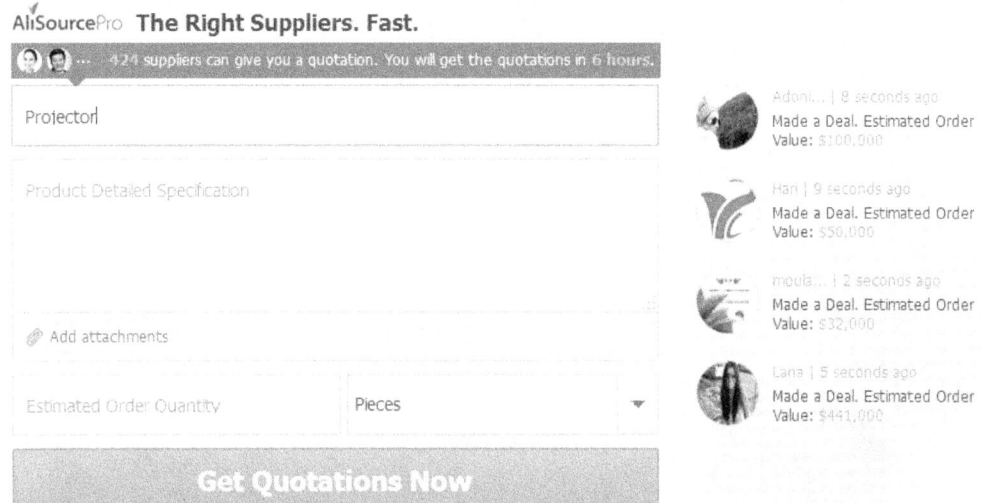

Quotations will be sent to your email account. The number of quotes will vary. It depends upon the type of product you are interested in. Within 24 hours I received this email (see image below) from Vicky. It is well written. I got of total of 6 responses from companies that make projectors.

Her email includes the number of years they have been in business, their phone, email, Skype name and company web site. This makes it easy for me to evaluate this business and based upon their rapid and thorough email I feel very good about this company. Notice how it is addressed to me personally (Sam Sommer). I only show the top of the email so it will fit on the page.

Dear Sam Sommer,
This is Vicky from Brilens,a professional LED projector manufacturer in China for 11 years.
I had sent a quotation to you from Alibaba.

We have projector for different occasions,like home theater,shool,boardroom,etc.
Could you tell me where you want to use the projector?
As all of our projector is LED,there's harmless for children.

Waiting for you reply.
Best regards,
Vicky(Sales)

CHANGSHA BRILENS TECHNOLOGY CO.,LTD.
Tel/Fax:86-0731-84770162
Mobile phone:86 13307489067
Email:sales2@brilens.com
Skype:pengyaoyuan
Company website:www.brilens.com

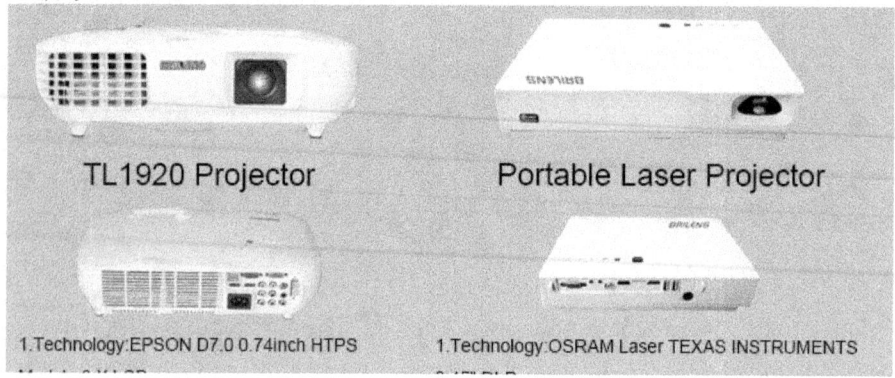

There are many ways of locating products and we will look at them later.

Getting back to the home page again, in the upper right is a tab labeled, "For Buyers". When you click on it, a box pops up (see below) and as you can see, there are many options available to you. There are three main headings: Source Products & Supplies, Trade Services and Community. The two left arrows point to Trade Assurance and Discussion Forums.

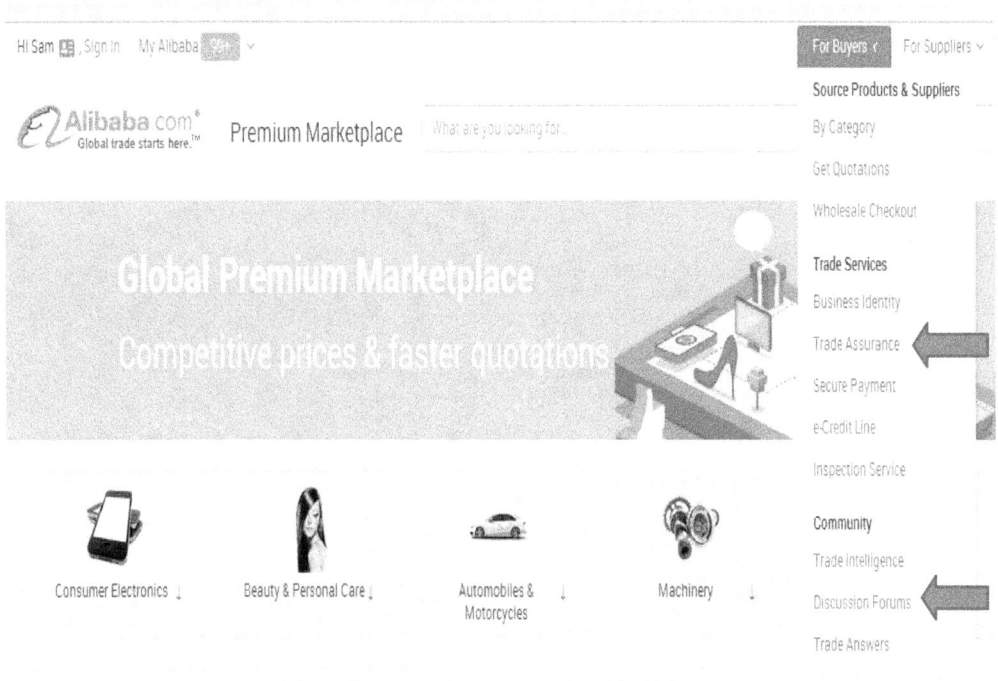

The arrows in the image above point to Trade Assurance and Discussion Forums. These are important, so let's look at them. If you click on Trade Assurance up pops this image, see below:

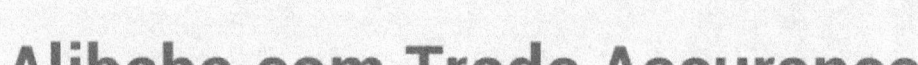 Trade Assurance

Alibaba.com Trade Assurance
Enabling businesses to trade with confidence

- ☑ Choose suppliers with a Trade Assurance Amount granted by Alibaba.com (based on trade history)
- ☑ 100% refund of the Trade Assurance Amount for orders not meeting agreed delivery or quality terms
- ☑ Supplier performance feedback system allows buyers to rate and review their experience

* It is a free service for both buyers and suppliers

According to Alibaba, Trade Assurance is:

"The Alibaba.com Trade Assurance program provides buyers with a number of trade safeguards which aim to both protect buyers' payment to suppliers, and to ensure suppliers fulfill their obligations regarding order delivery time and product quality. Based on a participating supplier's qualification status and its transaction volume in the past 6 months, Alibaba.com and/or its affiliated companies will grant the supplier a Trade Assurance Amount, which is an amount designated to protect buyers' payments made to suppliers.

If the participating supplier breaches certain terms of the Trade Assurance provisions as agreed in the relevant purchase order, Alibaba.com and/or its affiliated companies will compensate 100% of the Trade Assurance Amount to you. It is a free service for both buyers and suppliers."

> **1. Find participating suppliers & products displaying this icon**
>
> a. These suppliers agree to trade under the Alibaba.com Trade Assurance Service Rules.
>
> b. Based on the suppliers' qualifications and verified trade history, they are assigned a Trade Assurance Amount by Alibaba.com and/or its affiliated companies.
>
> c. The buyer must negotiate an agreed initial payment amount (deposit) with the supplier which should be covered up to the supplier's available Trade Assurance Amount.
>
> d. IMPORTANT NOTE: You will only be protected up to the Trade Assurance Amount as stated and agreed on the purchase order. The supplier's Trade Assurance Amount may be less than the deposit that you agree to pay to the supplier.

Trade Assurance, as it is explained in the image shown above, covers your deposit or initial payment amount and you must state this amount in the purchase order. So to protect yourself you have to make sure the supplier has enough Trade Assurance to cover your initial payment. We will revisit this topic later when we discuss payment methods.

The discussion forums (the second selection we pointed to) provides a convenient way to speak candidly with fellow buyers and ask questions and get help. These forums are in their infancy but they are candid and uncensored and you should take advantage of them.

This chapter took a brief look at the web site Alibaba.com and some important features were highlighted. More details will follow. When Jack Ma was interviewed on the day Alibaba went public, he emphasized that the little guy (buyers like us) were a priority for him.

The Alibaba.com Wholesale Site

As strange as it may seem, inside the Alibaba.com web site, is another web site, which is referred to as a "Wholesale Site". This does not mean that Alibaba.com itself is not wholesale, it's just a name they came up with to describe this sub web site which offers some features not found in the larger parent site.

The smaller, so called wholesale site, has fewer products but it does have features and benefits not found in the larger parent site. For example, in the larger site the only safe way to pay for product when you first place a purchase is through Trade Assurance. Trade Assurance was mentioned before and it will come up again, but for now, it is important to point out that if you do business with a company on the parent (larger) site you should only work with companies that offer Trade Assurance.

The smaller wholesale site does not have Trade Assurance. It has Secure Payment, which Alibaba formerly had available on its larger site when it was called Escrow, and it was the only safe way to buy-pay for product. Escrow is no longer available on the larger site but it is available on the wholesale site but the name was changed to Secure Payment. Take a look at this image below from the Alibaba web site:

What is Alibaba.com's Secure Payment service?

Alibaba.com Secure Payment aims to provide a safe payment service for all parties engaged in international trade. By partnering with an independent online payment platform (Alipay), Alibaba.com provides payment security to both buyers and suppliers.

Notice

From 22 Jan., 2015, Escrow Service change its name to Alibaba.com Secure Payment.

As you can see from the image above Alibaba states that on Jan 22, 2015 the word "Escrow" was changed to "Secure Payment". Secure Payment is only available on the smaller wholesale site as stated before. Alibaba explains Secure Payment this way:

Your money is held by Alipay, an independent online payment platform, until you confirm delivery. Once you have confirmed delivery, we will then notify Alipay to release the payment to the supplier.

If the supplier doesn't ship your order on time, or if you don't receive it and it is determined to be the fault of the supplier, you'll get your payment returned directly.

If the products you receive are significantly different from the product requirements agreed in the contract with the supplier, you may choose to receive a partial refund and also keep the products.

If your order hasn't arrived within the agreed time frame, or is delivered but isn't as described, contact the supplier via email or Trade Manager. Most suppliers will quickly resolve any issues.

If you were unable to resolve the issue with the supplier, you can submit a refund request by clicking Open Dispute before the applicable deadline. This function is available 5 days after the shipping date, and allows you to formally discuss solutions with the supplier.

If you are not satisfied with the supplier's solution, you can Escalate The Dispute to our Customer Service team. We will mediate between you and the supplier to resolve the problem.

Let's take a look at the smaller site, as this image below exemplifies:

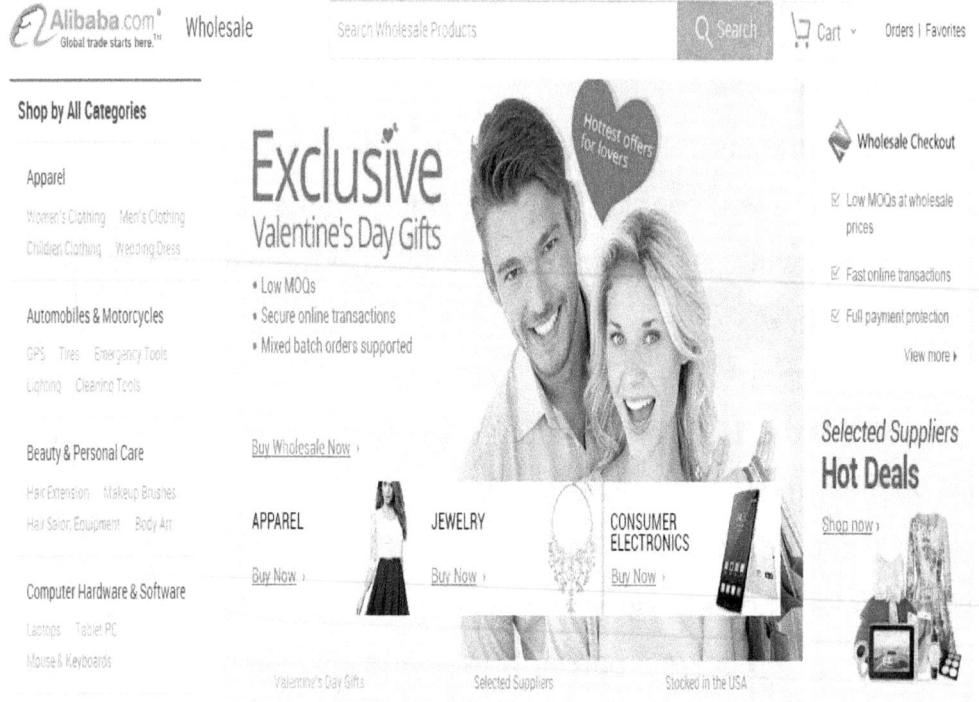

The site looks similar to Alibaba.com. It has many features that you should know about, in addition to Secure Payment. While it has less products than the bigger site, it still has a very generous selection. It is easy to navigate through the search tab or category tabs. The minimum order quantities range from 1 to about 100 so this makes it easier to make a small purchase (however some companies still have fairly large MOQ's).

It has a best selling feature on the min page, showing the items with the most orders and it has a trending feature, also on the main page, which can prove useful when you look for hot new products to sell.

Getting into the wholesale site is easy. When you are on the Alibaba.com main page, if you scroll down, on the left you will see:

Wholesale

Low MOQs

Secure Online Transactions
Buy It Now for Fast Dispatch

View More ›

Just click on "View More" or on the words and you will be taken into the wholesale site. The Hot Deals tab on the main page to the right is displayed below:

What is nice about the Hot Deals link is that it takes you to this section shown below:

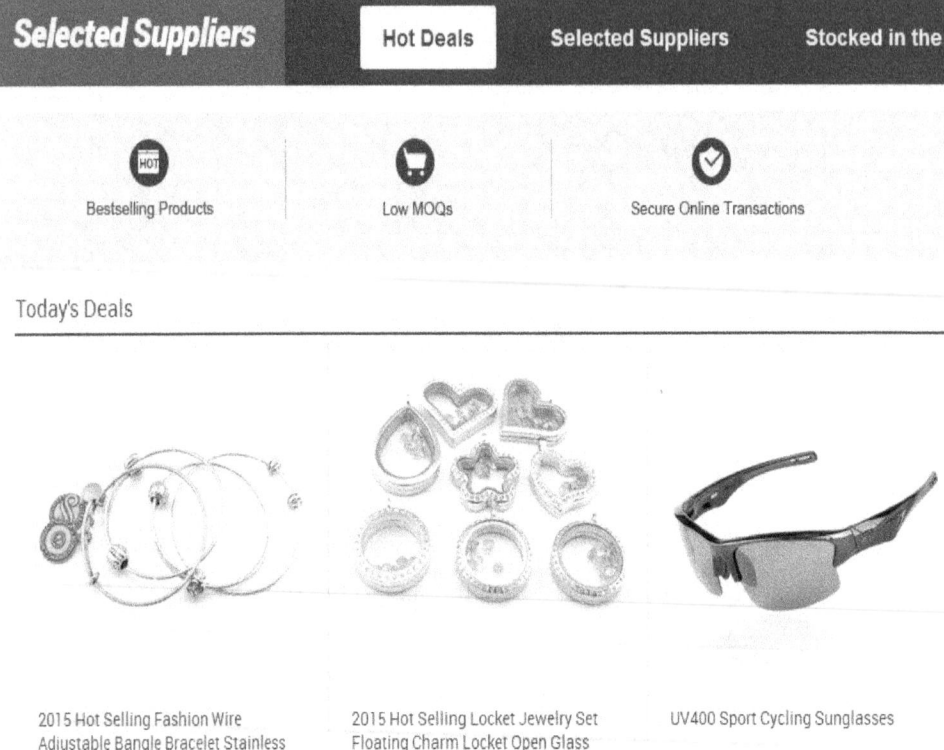

The image shown above, captures only part of the Hot Deals page, but does display what it looks like. Notice the tabs on top, in particular the one labeled: Stocked in the U.S. This is a great way to buy U.S. Based product and have it arrive quickly. Keep in mind that the Alibaba.com bigger web site displays vendors by country, so you can look for suppliers that are just from the U.S.

Also keep in mind that the products displayed on the wholesale site often have links back to the Alibaba.com site where more products, from the company whose product you are viewing, can be found.

Let's Look Inside AliExpress.com

AliExpress.com is a retail oriented web site that sells many, but not all of the products found on Alibaba.com and it has products not found on Alibaba.com. Many companies on Alibaba.com have AliExpress.com store fronts. AliExpress is easy to navigate and provides a convenient portal for ordering very small quantities of products for testing quality, and testing a product's sales potential. If you approach a company on Alibaba.com you should always ask if they have a store front on AliExpress.

The site has a nice look and feel to it and this screen capture image below, shows only a small part of the front page. Notice the categories and the weekly bestsellers (shows price and quantity sold). On top left I have circled the Super Deals tab, the Bestselling tab is next to it.

The super deals tab shows trending products that are being offered at steep discounts, usually 50% off. This is a good way to get your hands on some new product samples to test out.

After selecting the Bestselling tab you can see below what products are top sellers. The Samsung Galaxy S4 case has sold 4828 units in one week, #1 rated.

Another tab on the top of the main page of the web site is entitled "Buyer Protection". Buyer Protection helps safeguard the buying experience. If you do not receive your item or your item is not as described, you first try to work with the seller to resolve the issue. If this fails you contact AliExpress and they intervene. This system is very similar to eBay's Buyer Protection.

I think of the AliExpress web site as a way to buy very small quantities of a product you have interest in and want to test the waters with it. The prices are high and this site should not be used as a sourcing site for product ordering unless they have something you want that cannot be found anywhere else and the price is low enough to justify the purchase.

Is It A Good Product?

As you can see, the Alibaba web sites provide an easy and straightforward navigation experience. There is nothing mysterious or complex about them. It's very similar to steering your ship on the open sea. As long as there are no storms and no engine trouble all is well with the world. If only it were so simple.

So wherein lies the problem. The ocean analogy is well fitted to this discussion because Alibaba is so large that it can be thought of as a sea of products. Just like the ocean, there are sharks out there. As you can imagine, with over 2 million vendors to deal with, it is almost impossible for Alibaba, the company, to monitor and validate all of them. So how do we know who is trustworthy, and with over 35 million products on the site, which ones should we look at for resale? How do we hook and catch the good tasting fish and where do we find them?

Just like the fisherman, before you get in the boat and onto the water, you must be prepared. You need the best rod and reel and fishing line and the best bait. To make sales you need the best product. What characteristics do great products have?

What is the ideal product? Is there one that tops the list? Just imagine being the only person in the world selling the new Apple iPhone. This is a nice position to be in. Unfortunately it is impossible to be sitting on top of this gold mine. No worries though; there are lots a great products out there. What properties do they have in common?

First and foremost they must be readily available. This may seem obvious, but trust me, I have found great products that you just could not get your hands on. Let me give you an example. I found some pendants that were in great demand, but the company that makes them was no longer active and they could not be sourced. The lesson to be learned is, don't get mentally hung up, just move on to the next product.

A great product should be light weight and ideally small. This allows for easy handling, low shipping and return cost, easy inventory storage, inexpensive boxing or packaging (yes boxes cost money). No one likes a heavy product! Many sellers fail to fully factor shipping and packaging cost into the cost benefit analysis. Please do not get me wrong. There are many great products that sell well that are big and bulky, but why consider them if you are just getting started and don't have the room to store them, or for that matter, can't afford the inventory.

A great product should not be generic in nature. No one wants another silver or gold necklace, for example, but a silver or gold necklace that has a unique shape will attract attention. Even if you find a precious metal necklace at a great price, it won't sell if it lacks appeal.

For example, I have seen great rings, at great prices, sit on the shelf forever. Then, along comes a ring with a skull on it, and thousands are sold each month. It's the skull that makes the product sell, it is no longer just a ring.

Stay away from seasonal products and from fads. Certain products become very popular quickly because everyone wants one, then they disappear just as fast. Long term this approach does not work, examples include:

- Pogs
- Pokemon
- Flat-tops (The hairstyle, like Vanilla Ice had)
- The Walkman
- Acid Washed Jeans
- Converse High-Tops
- Snap Bracelets
- Tamagotchi (those little digital pet things)

Products that appeal to women are always winners. Women out buy men on eBay and Amazon probably 10 to 1 in many categories but not all. Why do you think Etsy is so popular? Products that appeal to a woman's vanity will always sell, assuming all factors are in place: price, size, margin, lack of competition etc…Products that are new and trending. Everyone likes to be the first to get one. I am not speaking about fads here.

Products under $10 never work. The margin for a $10 product is not favorable unless you can sell over 100 per week and this is very hard to do. Products over $100 make is very difficult to generate revenue because you just can't sell enough of them at that price point unless you can get thousands of visitors to your site each month. Remember, high priced products require lots of working capital.

Great products have strong emotional appeal. Products that address fear, safety, sexual desire, child issues (safety, health), protection. Examples include a new sexual device, such as vibrating lipstick, a new vitamin for children, a new product to protect women when they are out walking alone. Also, products that solve an immediate need, a better way to clean your floor, for example.

Products that have a tremendous markup are winners. For example, you pay $10 for it and it easily sells for $30, providing a $20 margin. Also, no matter how great a product is, it must have a good markup or profit margin, at least 100%. If it cost $10 you better be able to get $20 for it or you will loose long term. However, if you can sell hundreds per month, a small margin will generate good income. Don't confuse this with $10 and under products, that have almost no profit margin, and are hard to compete with.

Products that require a follow up purchase or a repeat order, are gold mines. As an example, you sell a wax warmer so hair can be removed, and the follow up product is the wax itself.

Stay away from products that have moving parts and require warranties. Sales may be brisk at first, but over time, if products start to fail, you will eat up profits quickly. Stay away from mass marketed products found at Walmart and other big box stores. Why try to compete on this level, it makes no sense.

Fragile products are very challenging. They require special handling and shipping and create too much anxiety. Let me give you an example. I sold a product made of resin that seemed very solid but I packed it carefully anyway. When it arrived at the customer's house, the legs were broken, yet there was no visible damage to the box. What I did not realize was that resin breaks in extremely cold weather and the box was sent to the mid west during the winter and temperatures were below zero.

Products sold in large quantities on eBay from Power Sellers are hard to compete with, but competition is not the issue. What makes it hard to sell against these big volume retailers is the level of traffic they have to their site. You may have the same product at a better price, but getting people to see it will result in frustration. In fact, so many people sell jewelry on Amazon, that you can no longer sell jewelry on their site, the market is too crowded. As an example, what comes to mind when you think of a 98 cent hamburger that tastes okay but is priced so low you are tempted to buy it? I think of McDonalds. Is it the best hamburger in the world? No, but at 98 cents you know exactly what you are getting and you know where to get it. So why go to the new burger store for their 99 cent product.

Good quality and low priced products have the potential to sell many units per day. If you have a new product and only sell one per week you may not be getting enough traffic to your listing. If you believe in the product stay with it. The buyers will eventual come and buy in volume. Adding new products regularly attracts interest.

Stay away from any product that has an image of a trademark or copyright on it: Disney Characters, Nike Logo, Apple Logo, etc... Products like these are boot legged, and you will be stopped if you try to sell them. For example, I noticed that many Chinese sellers use images from movies and place them on their products:

Here's an example of an Alibaba seller using the Disney characters in their product without their permission. What do you think will happen to you if you try and sell this wall decal?

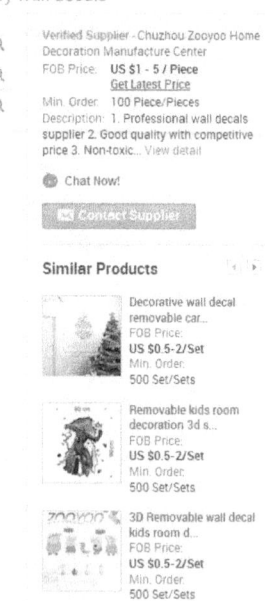

Clothing and fabric based products are in great demand and sell well online. But caution must be used here. Before stocking up on inventory you must test the products. Great products have been tested for washing damage, bleeding colors, shrinkage, size variations. Also test for smell on any products you buy – new shoes, for example, can sometimes smell badly.

In this chapter we looked at some traits associated with products that help increase and can decrease your chances of success. These are general rules, but I base this information on actual experience. Is there an exact formula to follow? No, but common sense is often pushed to the side when you see something that you think will be a winner and later find out it is not. There are some other factors to consider which will help you find the best products to sell and we will examine these as the chapters unfold.

Keep in mind that over one million families make a full time living selling on eBay, Amazon and Etsy. That means there are lots of good products out there and more waiting to be discovered.

Finding A Product To Sell

The ideal situation is to always sell things that you have familiarity with and enjoy using. A good example is fishing equipment. Why would you want to sell it if you have never fished? Do you know the difference between a bait casting reel and a spinning reel? So try to enter the sales arena with products that you are passionate about and have experience with.

I want to reveal a technique that I have used with great success and very few know about it. When traveling I always stop at gift shops, flea markets and convenience stores/gas stations, that sell souvenirs. Why? I can look at what is being sold and even find out the best selling items. I use a simple procedure to find this out.

I start by looking around the store. I notice if the clerk or manager is busy, if not, I strike up a conversation. I might say: "Wow, you have so many neat things here, it's amazing!" Then we exchange some words, simple conversation. Then I casually ask: "What do most people buy, what's most popular?"

This implies that you have interest in an item but you never state you want to buy anything. After they tell me I keep looking, maybe grab a drink or candy and pay for it, and then leave. Always say goodbye and thank them. Here's a real life example of how well this works.

On my way to Las Vegas I often stop at a gas station that sells hundreds of souvenirs. On one occasion I asked the clerk what the top seller is. I was told, and this surprised me, that it was the tin signs on the wall. They were priced at $16 on up, which is way more than their cost of around $1 on Alibaba.

The following images show what they look like:

Another sourcing technique that works well is looking for trends, what's hot. These web links can be very helpful. The Amazon best seller list for each category: This link, for example, is for toys:

http://www.amazon.com/gp/bestsellers/?ie=UTF8&camp=1789&creative=390957&linkCode=ur2&tag=startupbrosblog-20

An easy way to pull up the top 24 selling products on Amazon for any category or sub category is to place double brackets in the search box and then hit enter. Here are the two brackets, which I have separated so you can see them, but they should not have a space between them when you do your search [ ]. (one faces right, the other faces left)

Here are more links to best selling products on other web sites:

Hot picks on Kaboodle:

http://www.kaboodle.com/site/hot-picks

Shopzilla top searches:

http://www.shopzilla.com/top-searches

Top searches on mySimon:

http://www.mysimon.com/compare-top-searches

Some more Amazon links – For the "Movers" on Amazon:

http://www.amazon.com/gp/movers-and-shakers/?ie=UTF8&camp=1789&creative=390957&linkCode=ur2&tag=startupbrosblog-20

Amazon best sellers:

http://www.amazon.com/gp/bestsellers/?ie=UTF8&camp=1789&creative=390957&linkCode=ur2&tag=startupbrosblog-20

Always be on the lookout for hot and new items:
- Check your Sunday newspaper ad circulars for stores
- Check magazines
- Check flea markets
- Call stores to see what's hot – Staples, Dollar Stores e.g.
- Look at best sellers on Alibaba and AliExpress
- Check trend setters – Martha Stewart and others – look at their web sites
- Google "Hot New Items" or "Best Sellers"
- Ask friends who are always on top of trends
- Ask new moms what's hot

One of the best tools that I use for tracking and finding new products is a web site called: www.watchcount.com

Let's look at it. Without doubt it is one of the best ways to zero in on finding products to sell. The next image shows the main page:

It is so powerful and versatile. It allows you to search for the most watched items, for example, by selecting a category or keyword and the program goes into eBay and returns the top listings for that word or category showing the items that are being watched by the most people. It also shows most bids, keywords used most often, and so many other options.

Once you use it, you will quickly realize what people are most interested in, by product watched and bid on, and by key word search. So if you need to find products, use this tool, and if you have a product you can find out who else is selling it, what they are charging, and how many they are selling, and how fast they are being sold with WatchCount.

Here's an example. If you select the top eBay searches tab on the main page, then look in the "book" category, this is what comes up – see next image:

Top eBay Searches/Keywords

eBay Site: eBay.com   Page: 1
Categories: 267 **Books**

Category: Books [267]

	Related Searches	Alternatives
1	bible	easton press
2	nancy drew	books
3	signed	chess
4	alice in wonderland	stephen king
5	limited editions club	hunger games
6	goosebumps	folio society
7	manga	
8	franklin library	
9	catching fire	
10	diary of a wimpy kid	
11	sleaze	
12	hardy boys	
13	fifty shades of grey	
14	the great gatsby	
15	percy jackson	
16	little golden books	
17	50 shades of grey	
18	diary	
19	childrens books	
20	alcoholics anonymous	
21	occult	
22	magic tree house	
23	easton	
24	divergent	
25	mortal instruments	

Notice how the top keyword used in the Books Category is Bible. This information is very valuable. If you want to sell books, it's nice to know that more people are searching in the Book Category for the word "Bible" than anything else.

Look at the top searching in the Collectibles Category in the next image, and you thought Pokemon was a thing of the past.

Top eBay Searches/Keywords

eBay Site: eBay.com   Page: 1
Categories: 1 Collectibles

Category: Collectibles [1] (mw)

#	Related Searches	Alternatives
1	pokemon	knife
2	lighter	swarovski
3	porcelain sign	sword
4	sign	pokemon cards
5	meteorite	knives
6	coca cola	harry potter
7	order	
8	gas pump	
9	hello kitty	
10	doctor who	
11	thermometer	
12	lladro	
13	pen	
14	clock	
15	halloween	
16	hummel	
17	civil war	
18	one piece	
19	christmas ornaments	
20	vintage	
21	katana	
22	lot	
23	radio	
24	anvil	

Buying A Product To Sell

Once you locate some products that you are considering for resale you will need to find sources for them and get some samples. Never buy more than 1-3 samples when considering a new product. You have to test the waters before placing a large order. There are some basic procedures to follow when you are sourcing on Alibaba.com.

First use the Alibaba source tool located on the front page of the web site to locate companies that sell products you are interested in. At the same time search the Alibaba site for the product and see how many sources pop up. Let's look at these two options. The next image shows the sourcing tool on the front page of the site. Just click on the words: The most effective OEM/ODM & multi-category sourcing tool

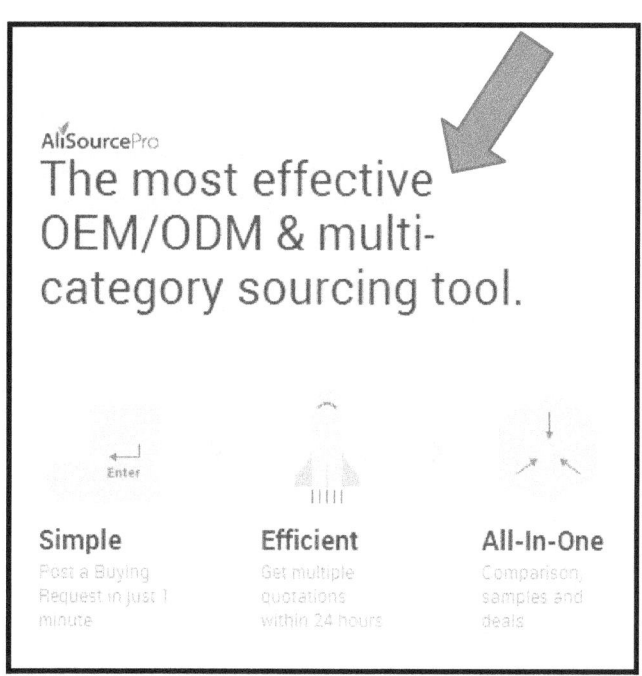

The next image pops up and you will enter a product to search for. You can search on a very generic name for a product, such as knife, or be more specific. The term "Tac-Force Knife" is an example of a specific knife that is a very big seller online. You will then be asked for a description and quantity. Just place a few words in, such as hunting knife, and any quantity, such as 100.

Once entered, you will see a confirmation message on the screen. Now sit back and wait. Within 1-2 days several quotes will come in, usually 2-12. While waiting for these quotes to come in, go into Alibaba and do your own product searches. This process is very easy:

On the main page of Alibaba.com type in "Hunting Knife" or "Tac-Force Knife" in the search bar: (I typed In Hunting Knife)

So after entering the words "Hunting Knife" you will see the search results. Below is what resulted from the search. I put a square on top of the 23,843 Products that the Alibaba search found for hunting knife – see next image:

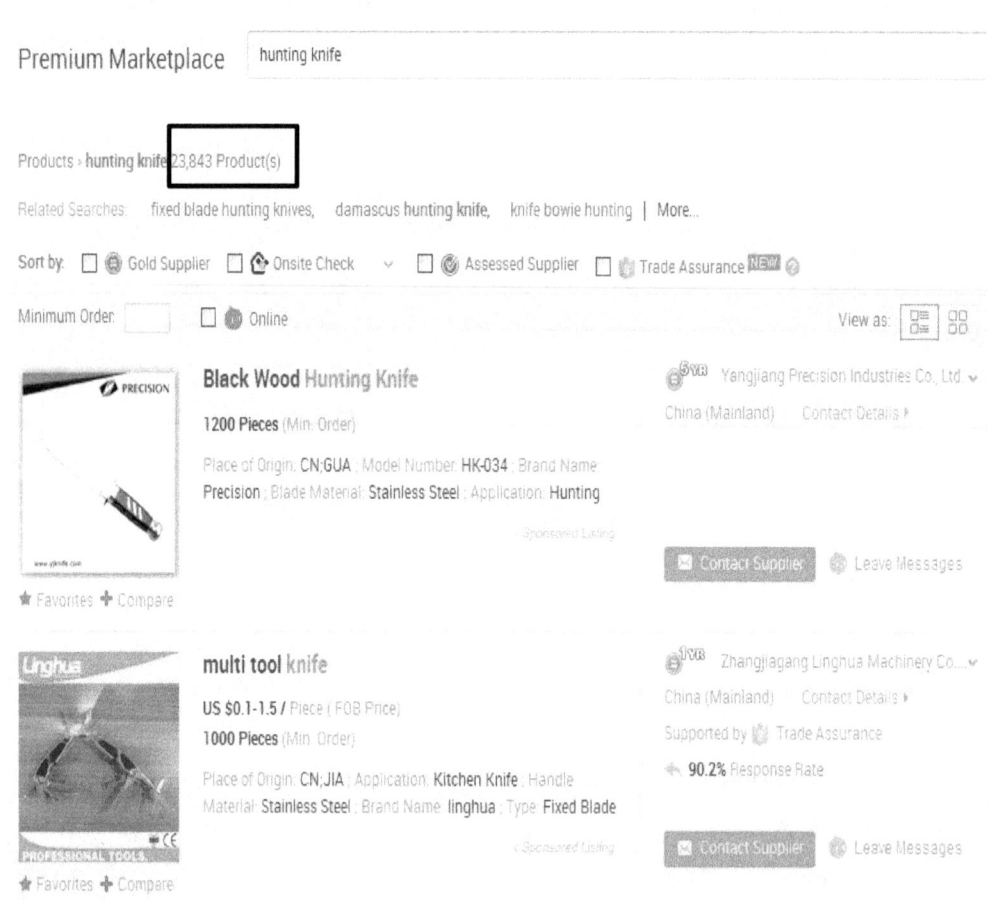

Way too many product options, so we need to narrow the range from 23,000 to a number we can work with. No one has time to scroll through 23,000 products. This is done buy checking boxes that allow us to select companies we can trust. Notice the 4 boxes on the image above – one for Gold Supplier, one for Onsite Check, one for Assessed Supplier and one for Trade Assurance.

In other words, only Gold Suppliers, who have been checked and assessed and offer trade assurance should be considered as possible vendors. After checking all four boxes the search is narrowed. Now there are 377 products to look at (see next image – arrow points to 377 Products found)

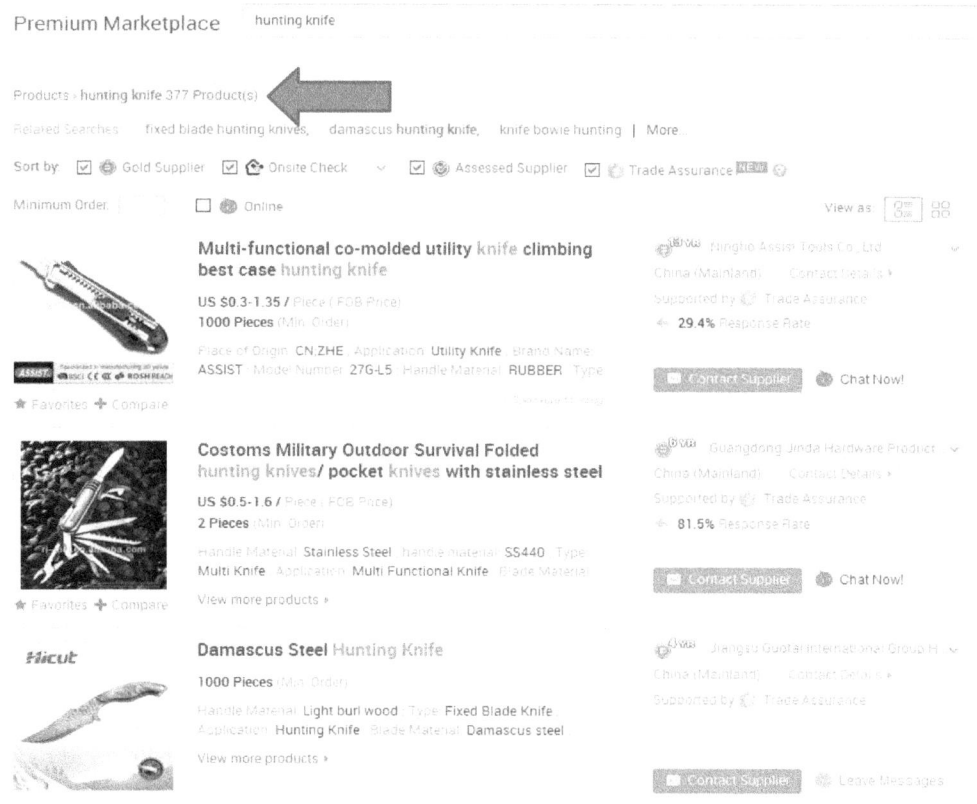

What's nice about this method of searching, and narrowing your results by checking boxes, you are left with fewer products to look at, and you know that the companies that sell them have met a standard of excellence.

Alibaba vendors that you should consider buying from have:

- 3 plus years gold membership (not one year or two years but at least three years)
- Are assessed and verified
- Usually have a web site and video
- Usually have good pictures showing their manufacturing facility
- Offer Trade Assurance
- Usually have an AliExpress store
- Answer their emails and answer questions clearly
- Usually will skype with you

Most scammers and companies looking to make a fast buck will never stay on the web site for more than 2 years, even if they pay the thousands of dollars, to become gold suppliers. So gold suppliers that have been selling for 3 years or more are pretty trustworthy.

You may be wondering what these terms mean: Gold Supplier, onsite check, assessed supplier, and trade assurance. It is very simple. A Gold Supplier is a company that pays Alibaba a fee each year to be listed as a Gold Supplier. The fee is large and only companies that have been in business for years and have strong cash flow can maintain this membership. It does not guarantee anything but it is a good sign. Onsite Check means that someone has gone to the location to verify that the business actually exists. This is usually done by a third party. Assessed suppliers have been checked by a third party inspection but this information is available for you to look at, and includes videos and pictures of the facility and more detail than just a check of the business location.

Trade assurance was explained before, but it bears repeating. It is an agreement between Alibaba and the company you do business with regarding money that Alibaba sets aside in case you have a dispute with the sale. This quote comes from the Alibaba web site:

"What is the Trade Assurance service ?

The Alibaba.com Trade Assurance program provides buyers with a number of trade safeguards which aim to both protect buyers' payment to suppliers, and to ensure suppliers fulfill their obligations regarding order delivery time and product quality. Based on a participating supplier's qualification status and its transaction volume in the past 6 months, Alibaba.com and/or its affiliated companies will grant the supplier a Trade Assurance Amount, which is an amount designated to protect buyers' payments made to suppliers.

If the participating supplier breaches certain terms of the Trade Assurance provisions as agreed in the relevant purchase order, Alibaba.com and/or its affiliated companies will compensate 100% of the Trade Assurance Amount to you. It is a free service for both buyers and suppliers."

When it comes time to buy and pay for samples and or products you must select trade assurance as your payment option otherwise you run the risk of loosing all your money. More details will follow. Remember, not all suppliers offer Trade Assurance. Do not do business with any that don't offer it. Also, remember that when you buy on the Wholesale site you are automatically protected by Secure Payment. The Wholesale site is the sub site found within Alibaba.com.

Evaluating Products

After zeroing in on some products that you have faith in and before investing money, you must try to determine the market potential for them, and this includes how well buyers react to their purchase. This is a fairly easy task to do, just go into any web site where the product is being sold and read the feedback and see how many are sold within a given time frame. Look in eBay, Amazon, AliExpress.com and Dhgate.com.

These sites have a feedback section and some show sales volume. Here's an example of how to do this. Let's look at a product and see how this evaluation works. The Tac-Force knife in the collectibles category on eBay is the number one selling product. WatchCount.com confirms this. I went into eBay and noticed that 6504 have been sold. If you click on the number 6504 (see figure below), you can see how often they are sold.

Here's a list of the sold knives for one day, 15 in total. So the question is: Can you make enough profit at this sales level and can you compete with this seller?

g***g (3855 ★)	US $12.99	1	Sep-28-14 22:02:54 PDT
s***u (12 ☆)	US $12.99	1	Sep-28-14 21:06:46 PDT
a***c (81 ★)	US $12.99	1	Sep-28-14 21:06:10 PDT
b***o (13 ☆)	US $12.99	1	Sep-28-14 20:41:08 PDT
i***- (2) 🔒	US $12.99	1	Sep-28-14 20:31:42 PDT
g***a (76 ★)	US $12.99	1	Sep-28-14 20:17:08 PDT
a***o (15 ☆)	US $12.99	1	Sep-28-14 18:55:05 PDT
u***2 (107 ☆)	US $12.99	1	Sep-28-14 17:11:49 PDT
b***o (13 ☆)	US $12.99	1	Sep-28-14 16:35:41 PDT
b***b (74 ★)	US $12.99	1	Sep-28-14 16:11:52 PDT
c***c (49 ☆)	US $12.99	1	Sep-28-14 12:07:13 PDT
4***h (23 ☆)	US $12.99	2	Sep-28-14 11:46:30 PDT
r***r (0) 🔒	US $12.99	1	Sep-28-14 10:15:43 PDT
t***m (19 ☆)	US $12.99	1	Sep-28-14 08:46:42 PDT
l***n (224 ☆)	US $12.99	1	Sep-28-14 05:26:26 PDT

I also checked the sellers feedback to see if any buyers had problems with the knives. Even though there were few of them, the issues that they raised caused me to be concerned about the quality of the knife, but not too concerned. To summarize, check sales volume per day or week, and feedback for any item you want to sell and you need to find out if the big sellers are selling them in volume. It is hard to compete with their traffic flow. In other words, if so many people look at their site for this item how will they find your knife?

I would also search for the knife on Amazon to see how many are being sold and what customers are saying about them and what price they are selling for. If I convinced myself that I could buy them at a low enough price and sell them at a price that let's me compete on eBay and Amazon and sell enough to make profit, I might consider this item.

Remember, do not run from competition, hit it head on. Offer free shipping, free replacement and 100% guarantee, including paying for return shipping and buyers will come a knocking on your door. That being said, there are thousands of better products out there than this knife.

Buying Samples

When you find a product to test and a vendor to buy it from, you must start out with a sample of 1-3 products. Most companies on Alibaba.com will sell a sample, but other ways to get samples include going to AliExpress.com and Dhgate.com. Many of the bigger companies on Alibaba will give you a sample for free. You just pay shipping. It is important to understand how samples and smaller items can be shipped so you do not overpay for shipping.

Most of us are unaware of a special deal that the U.S. Post Office, eBay and China has worked out. They set up extremely low shipping rates for Chinese companies so these suppliers can ship to the U.S. for almost nothing. The chart that follows shows these "ePacket" rates:

Weight	e-Packet Rate $	eBay USPS First Class parcel $	USPS Priority Mail- Retail (Zone 7) $
1 oz	0.98	1.64	
2 oz	0.98	1.64	
3 oz	1.28	1.64	
4 oz	1.70	1.81	
5 oz	2.13	1.98	
6 oz	2.55	2.15	
7 oz	2.98	2.31	
8 oz	3.40	2.48	
9 oz	3.75	2.65	
10 oz	3.75	2.82	
11 oz	3.90	2.99	
12 oz	4.25	3.14	
13 oz	4.61	3.28	
1lb	5.67		5.9
2 lb	11.34		9.45
3 lb	17.01		11.8
4 lb	22.68		15
4.4 lb	25.00		17.25

ePacket allows Chinese sellers to ship to the U.S. for extremely low rates. For example, an 8oz or ½ pound item costs $3.40 to travel all the way from China to the U.S. and when it gets here the USPS delivers it as a first class package. It takes 5-10 days to go from China to your door here in the U.S. Keep these rates in mind when ordering samples, so you are not cheated. Notice the rate for a 1oz packet, only 98 cents.

Larger weights can be shipped using any of the major carriers, such as UPS, FedEx, DHL and others. The vendors usually know the rates and can recommend the best rate and carrier. The best way to protect yourself from high rates is to get quotes for the same product and quantity from multiple vendors. I asked two different vendors for shipping rates for the exact same product, same weight, and one told me $85 and the other said $350 (both were using the same carrier, DHL). One was trying to cheat me at $350. You can of course go to the shipping web sites and calculate charges yourself.

When ordering samples you can expect to pay a premium but always negotiate with the seller. As stated, some will send a sample for free, you just pay shipping. If for example, they offer to send you 3 pieces for $45, including shipping, ask them if they can do it for $30. Tell them another company is offering it at that rate and see what they say. They always tell you they will credit you for the samples, once you place a bigger order, but don't be taken advantage of.

Remember everything is negotiable, especially the price and quantity. What we fail to realize when we buy from China is the price manipulation that takes place. One U.S. dollar is worth about 6.5 Chinese Yuan. What can $1 or 6.5 Yuan buy in China? Let's look at $1.50 or 10 Yuan as an example. With 10 Yuan, you can get 6 cucumbers, 4 apples, 6 tomatoes and 5 onions. In the U.S. you would spend about $8 for these items. So a $1.50 profit in China is like $8 profit in the U.S.

When your samples arrive test them out. Look at them, inspect them, wash them, try them or do whatever you have to do to make sure they work and look good. Then place them for sale on eBay, Amazon and Etsy and see how they do.

Don't worry about getting your money back for the price of the samples. Just try to sell the items and see how customers like them. I have noticed that there are many types of companies on Alibaba. There are the small ones, looking to make a fast buck and these are the ones that you will have trouble communicating with. Then there are large reputable companies that will skype with you and have a good command of the English language. Many of these better companies have representatives in the U.S. and in other countries. It is much easier to speak with someone on the phone than emailing or skyping. So ask if they have a rep in your country.

The key to success is to take your time and find good quality products from reliable vendors. Don't be in a hurry. Do your research and when you find a product to sell the reward will justify the dues that are paid.

Paying For Your Products

What troubles me is the fact that horror stories still show up online from time to time, about victims of Alibaba supplier fraud. I recently read about one family who lived in the Caribbean. They lost over $100,000 purchasing from an Alibaba company that ended up stealing their money.

There is no reason why this should happen to you. There are so many ways to protect yourself. If you only do business with gold suppliers who have had gold status for at least three years, this in and of itself, would be a great safeguard. And if you use Trade Assurance wisely on Alibaba.com and Secure Payment on the smaller wholesale site and Buyer Protection on AliExpress that will ad more layers of safety.

The first thing you should always do when considering order placement is research and communication with your supplier. Does your supplier have a video, has their factory been checked and assessed? Do they communicate with you in a timely fashion and clearly? Do they answer your questions completely. Can they list companies that buy from them? This is not game changer, but if they have good references, it helps.

Remember, Alibaba is not at fault. With 2 million companies using their portals they cannot monitor all activity in a timely fashion. The bad sellers get thrown off the web site, but not right away, so if you do business with them you could be their first and maybe only victim.

Alibaba is constantly trying to make the buying experience a better one. I always suggest you buy 1-3 samples before ever placing a big order. If the company won't work with you on the sample order, you know they are fraudulent.

Another way to check on a potential supplier is to look at their web site. Do they even have a web site? If not, be very careful. What products do they sell on the site? Do they have one product or many products? Do their products fall into many different categories, indicating that they don't make them, they just buy and resell them? This is not necessarily a bad thing, but it should become part of the decision process.

Please keep in mind that you often find the same product listed on many Alibaba.com supplier's web pages or store fronts. Why is this? Many Alibaba vendors do not actually make the products they sell. They buy them from companies that manufacture them and only sell them wholesale in bulk to Alibaba.com resellers. Even if you find the manufacturer you may not be able to buy from them directly.

After you decide to place an order, big or small, and you are using Trade Assurance or Secure Payment or Buyer Protection you still have to pay using some type of payment method. Depending upon which web site you are using, the payment type may change. But in general, no matter what form of protection Alibaba.com is offering you should never pay by bank transfer, money order, Western Union. A company that demands a bank transfer, for example, cannot be trusted.

Even though your payment is going directly to Alibaba.com when you use Secure Payment, for example, it is better to use a credit card so you can dispute any charges, if need be. That being said, I encourage you to invest in a credit or debit card that is not tied to your bank directly. One that has little money in it or a small credit limit, so if something goes wrong you are protected.

For example, if you have a debit Visa card with no direct tie to any bank account and you keep $100 in it as a rule, this would be a good card to use for a small sample order. Once you do business with a company and see how it goes, you can increase the order size. Please keep in mind that most Alibaba vendors are honest, so don't become overly concerned, but protect yourself as much as possible.

Branding Increases Cash Flow

Most sellers on eBay and Amazon and other retail sites do not understand what branding is and why it is important. Branding is a very simple concept to understand and take advantage of. In fact, everyone has purchased a branded product. We spoke about McDonalds earlier. A Big Mac is an example of a branded product. Yes it just a hamburger with two beef patties and sauce but everyone knows what it is and who sells it.

When I use the term branding with regard to selling online I refer to it this way: You are branding when you take a product, usually an existing product, and put your name on the product and or on the box that holds the product. Most branded products on eBay and Amazon are products that are already made for a large company and only sold with the company name on the box and product. But many suppliers, and some who even sell to large companies that brand the products, will sell them to you, and they will put your company name on the box and possibly the product. The supplier has the rights to the product but they agree to let you sell it under your label. Most large manufacturing companies let other companies resell their product under the retail sellers name. This happens in the food industry. So when you buy product under the store name, the product is made by someone else but sold as a store product. The same product may show up in other food stores under the name of that food store.

So why do this? Branding makes it possible for customers to recognize the product and associate it with a certain level of quality and a fair price. As a small seller on eBay or Amazon, you can find a product to sell and put your name on the box and or product and build a following. No one else can copy you. They cannot use your name. So what happens is that your customers associate your name with a certain level of quality and refer others to your listing, looking for the product with your name on it.

A good example of a brand name is Vizio TVs and Vizio products. Many companies sell Vizio products to consumers, including Vizio. What happens on Amazon, for example, if you look for a Vizio 5.1 Sound Bar, is that the same listing comes up on top all the time. The Vizio Sound Bar made by Vizio is always on top, while the ones that Walmart and Best Buy and others sell appear in a lower position in the search results. Vizio will not let you take their sound bar and put your name on it. If you want to sell it and compete with them you have to sell their brand named product.

But you can find products that are not branded and put your name on them. Once you build up a following, customers will always look for your name and associate the name with quality and a fair price. This gives you an advantage.

You will notice on many product listings on Alibaba.com that the companies that offer the product will private label or brand for you if the quantity is right. Here's the Vizio Sound Bar (shown below). Every time you search on Amazon for this product, the one sold by Vizio, and fulfilled by Amazon, comes up in the number one position even though other companies sell it, and at times have it for a better price,

How eBay Sellers Make Millions Sourcing Alibaba Products

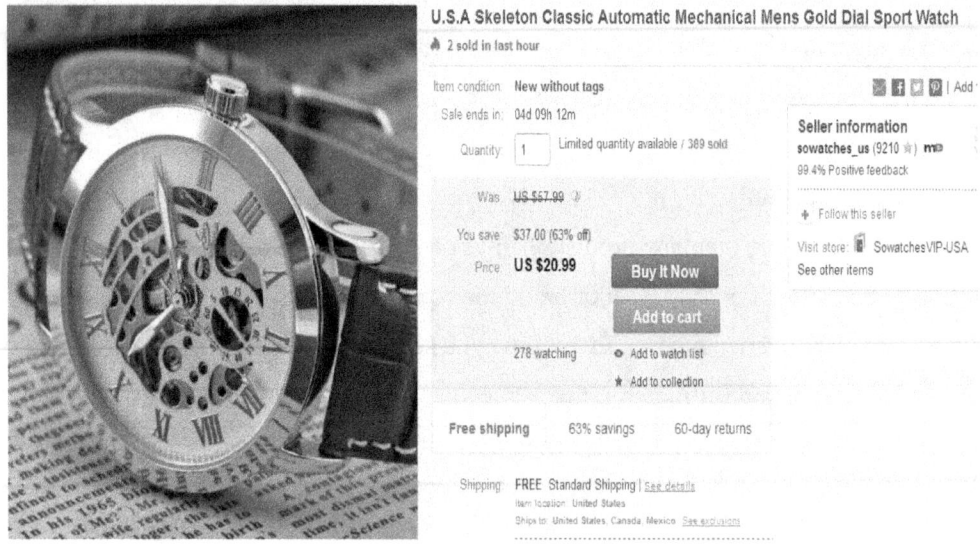

Here's a classic example of an eBay seller who sources product from Alibaba. It is fairly easy to estimate how much money they make. Take a close look at the watch listed on eBay in the picture above. Almost 400 have been sold and in just one day almost 60 were sold. I clicked on the number 389 next to the word sold and eBay lists all the sales per day. So what do they pay for them and where do they get them?

I went into Alibaba and found one vendor who sells the watch. Here is their listing on the Alibaba site:

This is the exact same watch (notice the front design and red handle).They offer it for a range of $1 - $20. I do not know what this eBay seller paid for the watch. Let's assume that they paid $8 and are making $6 profit per watch after paying for shipping and eBay fees. In just one day they made almost $500 profit (60 times 8). I am sure that there are other vendors on Alibaba that also have the watch and may even have it for less money.

Now multiply this product by the other products this eBay seller has and by the profit the other products make. You can see how it can add up to millions quickly. I have seen eBay Power Sellers who sold 50,000 units of a product in just a few weeks and made $2-3 profit per unit in that short time period, adding up to over $100,000 in those few short weeks.

Conclusion

The task of finding products for resale on eBay, Amazon and Etsy may at first glance, seem overwhelming. But with some practice, patience and smart thinking (following the guidelines outlined in this book) you can achieve success. There are always new products coming along and hard working sellers take advantage of them. There is no magic bullet, you must pay your dues.

Paying your dues simply means having the patience it takes to become a destination for buyers on any of the major online sites we spoke about. Attracting people to your online listing and getting them to buy your products requires that you offer items that have appeal, are fairly priced, and most importantly, the offering comes with great service. You must ship quickly, have solid packaging and always refund or replace when customers have issues. A happy customer is a returning customer and a referring customer.

With over 35 million products to choose from, Alibaba is a gold mine in the making and if you do a little digging, the result will be well worth the effort. Remember, there are over one million people selling on eBay and other online portals who make a full time income. Many make millions per year.

Why not add your name to the list?

www.ingramcontent.com/pod-product-compliance
Lightning Source LLC
Chambersburg PA
CBHW071816170526
45167CB00003B/1327